Pebble® Plus

Bugs, Bugs, Bugs!

Praying Mantises

by Margaret Hall

Consulting Editor: Gail Saunders-Smith, PhD

Consultant: Gary A. Dunn, MS, Director of Education
Young Entomologists' Society Inc.
Lansing, Michigan

Capstone
press®

Mankato, Minnesota

D1405338

Pebble Plus is published by Capstone Press,
1710 Roe Crest Drive, North Mankato, Minnesota 56003.
www.capstonepub.com

Books published by Capstone Press are manufactured with
paper containing at least 10 percent post-consumer waste.

Library of Congress Cataloging-in-Publication Data
Hall, Margaret, 1947–
    Praying mantises/by Margaret Hall.
    p. cm.—(Pebble plus: Bugs, bugs, bugs!)
    Includes bibliographical references (pg. 23) and index.
    ISBN-13: 978-0-7368-2590-0 (hardcover)   ISBN-10: 0-7368-2590-8 (hardcover)
    ISBN-13: 978-0-7368-5098-8 (softcover pbk.)   ISBN-10: 0-7368-5098-8 (softcover pbk.)
    1. Praying mantis—Juvenile literature. [1. Praying mantis.] I. Title. II. Series.
QL505.9M35H25 2005
595.7'27—dc22   2003024966

Summary: Simple text and photographs describe the physical characteristics and habits of praying mantises.

Editorial Credits
Sarah L. Schuette, editor; Linda Clavel, series designer; Kelly Garvin, photo researcher; Karen Hieb, product
    planning editor

Photo Credits
Bruce Coleman Inc./J&L Waldman, 12–13; Karen McGougan, 8–9
Minden Pictures/Gerry Ellis, 18–19
Pete Carmichael, 4–5, 6–7, 15, 16–17
Robert & Linda Mitchell, cover, 1, 11
Stephen McDaniel, 20–21

Note to Parents and Teachers

The Bugs, Bugs, Bugs! series supports national science standards related to the diversity of life and heredity. This book describes and illustrates praying mantises. The images support early readers in understanding the text. The repetition of words and phrases helps early readers learn new words. This book also introduces early readers to subject-specific vocabulary words, which are defined in the Glossary section. Early readers may need assistance to read some words and to use the Table of Contents, Glossary, Read More, Internet Sites, and Index/Word List sections of the book.

Word Count: 96
Early-Intervention Level: 11

Printed in the United States of America in North Mankato, Minnesota.
012013   007153R

Table of Contents

Praying Mantises

What are praying mantises?

Praying mantises are insects.

How Praying Mantises Look

Praying mantises are about
the size of a child's finger.
Praying mantises have
six legs.

Many praying mantises have
green or brown bodies.
Praying mantises can also
be pink, white, or yellow.

Some praying mantises
look like leaves or flowers.
Praying mantises sit
very still.

What Praying Mantises Do

Praying mantises turn
their heads from side
to side. Their heads
look like triangles.

Praying mantises fold
their front legs together.

Praying mantises grab other animals to eat.

Praying mantises bite
and chew with strong jaws.

Praying mantises clean
themselves after they eat.

Glossary

fold—to bring together, or to bend close to the body; praying mantises fold their legs together; the action makes the mantis look like it is praying.

grab—to take hold of something quickly; praying mantises stay very still waiting for other animals to eat; they quickly grab the animals.

insect—a small animal with a hard outer shell, six legs, three body sections, and two antennas; most insects have wings.

jaw—a part of the mouth used to grab, bite, and chew

Read More

Frost, Helen. *Praying Mantises.* Insects. Mankato, Minn.: Pebble Books, 2001.

Hipp, Andrew. *The Life Cycle of a Praying Mantis.* The Life Cycles Library. New York: PowerKids Press, 2002.

Scholl, Elizabeth J. *Praying Mantis.* Bugs. San Diego: Kidhaven Press, 2004.

Internet Sites

FactHound offers a safe, fun way to find Internet sites related to this book. All of the sites on FactHound have been researched by our staff.

Here's how:

1. Visit *www.facthound.com*

2. Type in this special code **0736825908** for age-appropriate sites. Or enter a search word related to this book for a more general search.

3. Click on the **Fetch It** button.

FactHound will fetch the best sites for you!

Index/Word List